STEM IN AUTO RACING

SportsZone
print of Abdo Publishing
odopublishing.com

BY MEG MARQUARDT

ABDOPUBLISHING.COM

Published by Abdo Publishing, a division of ABDO, PO Box 398166, Minneapolis, Minnesota 55439.
Copyright © 2018 by Abdo Consulting Group, Inc. International copyrights reserved in all countries.
No part of this book may be reproduced in any form without written permission from the
publisher. SportsZone™ is a trademark and logo of Abdo Publishing.

Printed in the United States of America, North Mankato, Minnesota
102017
012018

THIS BOOK CONTAINS
RECYCLED MATERIALS

Cover Photo: Silvia Izquierdo/AP Images
Interior Photos: Silvia Izquierdo/AP Images, 1; Michael Probst/AP Images, 4–5; Shizuo Kambayashi/
AP Images, 7; Logan Whitton/NKP/AP Images, 8; Phelan M. Ebenhack/AP Images, 11; Butch Dill/
AP Images, 12–13; Rey Del Rio/NASCAR/Getty Images, 15; Shutterstock Images, 17; John Raoux/
AP Images, 18; Peter Fox/Getty Images Sport/Getty Images, 20–21; Getty Images Publicity/Getty
Images, 22; Luca Bruno/AP Images, 25; Hoch Zwei/picture-alliance/dpa/AP Images, 26; Darrell
Ingham/Getty Images Sport/Getty Images, 28–29; Saso Domijan/Sipa/AP Images, 30; Jeffrey Vest/
Icon Sportswire, 33; Graham Hughes/The Canadian Press/AP Images, 35; Ned Jilton II/Kingsport
Times-News/AP Images, 36; Emmanuel Dunand/AFP/Getty Images, 38–39; Jeff Siner/Charlotte
Observer/MCT/Tribune News Service/Getty Images, 41; iStockphoto, 42; Alberto Saiz/AP Images, 44

Editor: Arnold Ringstad
Series Designer: Maggie Villaume
Content Consultant: Dr. Greg Kremer, Robe Professor and Chair, Mechanical Engineering,
      Ohio University

PUBLISHER'S CATALOGING-IN-PUBLICATION DATA
Names: Marquardt, Meg, author.
Title: STEM in auto racing / by Meg Marquardt.
Description: Minneapolis, Minnesota : Abdo Publishing, 2018. | Series: STEM in sports | Includes
      online resources and index.
Identifiers: LCCN 2017946907 | ISBN 9781532113468 (lib.bdg.) | ISBN 9781532152344 (ebook)
Subjects: LCSH: Automobile racing--Juvenile literature. | Sports sciences--Juvenile literature. |
      Physics--Juvenile literature.
Classification: DDC 796.72--dc23
LC record available at https://lccn.loc.gov/2017946907

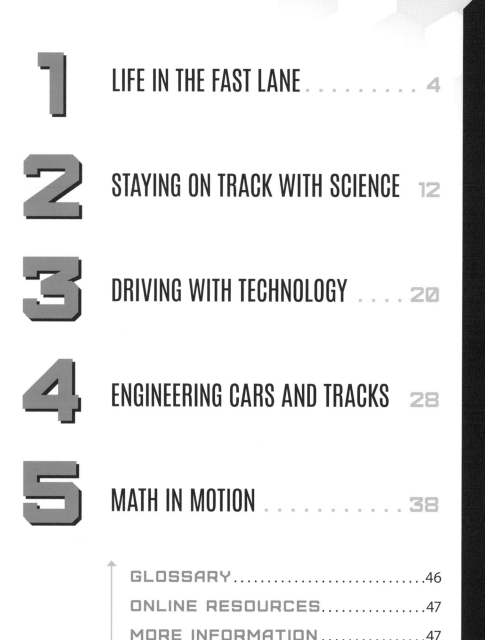

TABLE OF CONTENTS

Michael Schumacher zooms around a corner on a track in Germany.

1

LIFE IN THE FAST LANE

The pack of cars races around the track at almost 200 miles per hour (320 km/h). The final turn is coming up. The second-place driver looks for an opportunity to overtake the leader. He knows he has to time his move perfectly. The turn comes, and the driver ahead makes a major mistake. The first-place driver goes into the turn too widely, veering off to the track's outer edge. The second-place driver takes his chance.

He knows that hugging the inside of the track will help him close the gap. His car has been specially designed for just this move. Its tires grip the road with just enough friction to stop him from losing control but not so much as to slow him down. As he presses down the accelerator pedal, the car's engine takes in more fuel to give him a boost of power at just the right moment to speed past the leader. He takes the lead at the home stretch, racing down the last straightaway to beat every other car to the finish line. The driver's skill was a crucial component in this race. But it was not the only factor. The winning team took science, technology, engineering, and math (STEM) into account to achieve a first-place finish.

RACING CARS

Auto racing is one of the most popular sports in the world. For many decades, fans have come to tracks to

Team engineers and technicians make careful adjustments to cars with STEM principles in mind.

cheer on drivers who have the skills to go fast while staying in control. The first auto race took place in 1894. The top speeds in that first race were only 10.2 miles per hour (16.4 km/h). Now, some cars can go more than 20 times as fast. Around the world, races continue to showcase speed and skills.

Auto racing comes in many forms. Each type of race requires specially built cars that can handle different demands. Formula 1 (F1) cars have to handle twisty, curvy tracks. These low, sleek vehicles look

Most NASCAR tracks, including Homestead-Miami Speedway in
Florida, have oval shapes.

very different from ordinary cars. NASCAR vehicles do
not face many twists and turns. Instead, they usually
drive in oval shapes. However, they reach incredible
sustained speeds. IndyCar races happen on a mix of
oval tracks and more complicated road circuits. F1,
NASCAR, and IndyCar races are considered sprints. Races
last approximately two hours. Endurance races are a
different type of competition. Cars in these races have to
be sturdy enough to withstand up to 24 hours of racing.

STEM IN ACTION

At every turn, STEM fields play key roles in auto racing.
Race cars do all the things a normal car does. They
accelerate, make turns, brake, and are designed to

protect their drivers in the event of a crash. However, competitive racing cars are lighter and more powerful. They need responsive steering and a suspension tuned to the specific race conditions and track.

Science helps auto racing specialists understand the conditions of the road. They study how at high speeds even something as thin as air can slow down a car. The cars are built to be extremely aerodynamic. This means they are designed so that air resistance slows them down as little as possible. Scientists also use chemistry to create better racing fuel.

A driver has a huge amount of technology at her fingertips. An F1 steering wheel looks like a video game controller. Buttons and knobs dictate everything from switching gears to injecting fuel into the engine. With so much technology, a driver can make quick adjustments with a flick of the wrist.

Engineering helps race car designers in their quest to create the perfect car. Fuel tanks are extra strong to help prevent explosions. Seat belts hold the driver in place much better than in a normal car. The driver's outfit even has special clips that help protect the head and neck from damage.

Pit crews use math to determine the best tire pressure for each race. They also have to calculate how much fuel to add at a pit stop, getting the car back on the track in seconds. Numbers matter to drivers, too. Inside the car, they have to be able to read the road. They must know what speed to hit when entering and exiting a turn.

Science, technology, engineering, and math all go hand in hand in auto racing. They help drivers accelerate off the starting line, zoom around tight corners, and stay safe while doing so. Powerful cars going at high speeds can lead to dangerous crashes. However, engineers and scientists have created all sorts of safety precautions. STEM keeps auto racing not only fast and fun but also safe for drivers and fans.

The high speeds and extreme forces in auto racing make well-engineered safety gear essential.

The shapes of racing cars are designed to reduce drag and maximize top speeds.

2

STAYING ON TRACK WITH SCIENCE

Auto racing has an invisible foe: air. Air is one of the biggest obstacles to going fast. It pushes back against any object in motion. If that object isn't going too fast, the push doesn't have much impact. But at high speeds, the force needed to push air out of the way becomes a problem. This phenomenon is called air resistance, or drag. As engineers and scientists studied drag, they realized cars had to be designed differently. The shape of cars today has everything to do with fighting drag.

DRAG

Even though the air might feel empty, it is actually made up of molecules. These molecules include the gases people breathe. They are tiny, but these molecules can still cause a lot of problems in racing.

A fast-moving car faces constant resistance from these molecules. They push back against the car, causing drag and slowing it down. As a car speeds up, the power needed to overcome drag increases. This makes a car less efficient. The engine has to pump out more power to overcome the force of air. That means more fuel is used and the car can't go quite as fast.

The problem of drag has shaped the auto racing industry. It has also shaped the cars. In order to combat

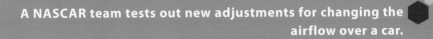
A NASCAR team tests out new adjustments for changing the airflow over a car.

air resistance, race car manufacturers design the cars to cut through air. They minimize the area that needs to push through the air, and they streamline the car's shape. The front and sides are curved, allowing air to flow smoothly around the car. The bottom is extremely low to the ground. This forces air to mostly flow over the top of the car, helping keep the car as close to the track as possible.

However, air still tries to sneak under the car. When a car turns or starts to spin because of a crash, more air can get underneath. When that happens, the car can actually lift off the track. Once the wheels leave the road, the car goes out of control.

To prevent cars from flipping, manufacturers developed a part called a wing. It is located at the front and rear of F1 cars. It works like an upside-down airplane wing. Rather than providing the lift that carries airplanes into the sky, it pushes down to keep cars on the ground. This helps keep the tires on the track.

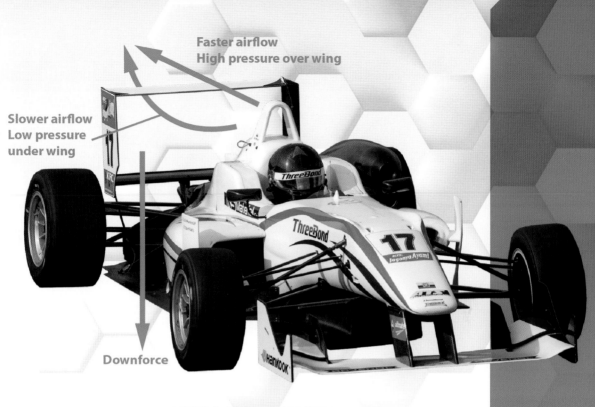

Faster airflow
High pressure over wing

Slower airflow
Low pressure
under wing

Downforce

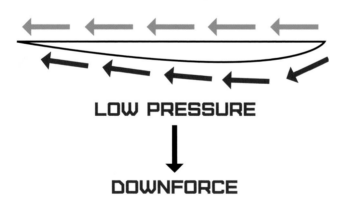

HIGH PRESSURE

LOW PRESSURE

DOWNFORCE

Along with tire friction, downforce keeps the car's tires close to the ground. A race car is built to optimize downforce. An F1 car has a rear wing that redirects turbulent air. Instead of that air moving in multiple directions, the wing forces that air upward. When the air moves up, it exerts a force in the opposite direction. That pushes down on the car, creating downforce.

At NASCAR races, fuel is stored in special cans.

FUELING SPEED

Chemistry plays a big part in racing as well. Race cars use fuel that's specially made for the high demands of going fast for a long time. In NASCAR, the fuel is called Green E15. Its color is actually green. Each gallon of fuel is 85 percent gasoline and 15 percent ethanol.

Gasoline is a fossil fuel. It is made by processing oil found underground. The oil forms over millions of years from the remains of ancient plants and animals. Ethanol is an alcohol. It can be made from corn.

KEEPING DRIVERS HYDRATED AND FED

Races can go on for hours. During that time, drivers might get hungry or thirsty. That's why nutrition science plays a big role in racing. To keep their energy up, some drivers stash protein bars in the car. They also have a special hydration system. The system allows them to take sips of sports drinks during the race. A ventilation system blows fresh air into the car. These systems can be lifesavers, because the inside of the car can reach 140 degrees Fahrenheit (60°C). Such temperatures would cause a driver to sweat and become dehydrated.

Racing team engineers study the data that is
streaming in from their car.

3

DRIVING WITH TECHNOLOGY

Modern auto racing involves huge amounts of data. Crews can gather information in real time that helps shape each and every race. Data also drives the technology of the auto racing field. Knowing how well a car is running can influence the new types of technology that is needed to make even better cars.

TELEMETRY

Many race cars are fitted with sensors. These sensors give the pit crew real-time

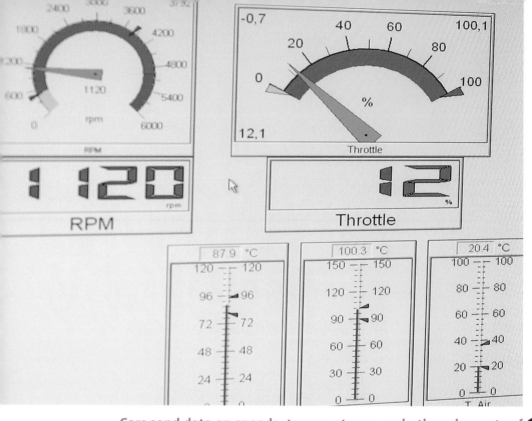

Cars send data on speeds, temperatures, and other elements of their performance to race teams.

information about the car's performance. The system that gathers and transmits this data is known as telemetry.

Telemetry provides information on everything from fuel levels to tire pressure to acceleration. An IndyCar can have up to 80 sensors. A lot of this data is examined after the race. Teams can study how the data changes during a racing season to see which tracks they are having problems on. They can identify areas for improvement, such as adjusting the fuel injection into the engine.

Another aspect of telemetry is that racing fans can get sneak peeks into their favorite cars. Streaming and mobile apps allow fans to follow the streams of data collected by cars. They can even listen in on drivers talking to their crews during a race.

THE STEERING WHEEL

Some race cars, such as those in NASCAR, have a fairly normal steering wheel. Others have wheels with a handful of buttons. But some drivers have a whole computer right at their fingertips.

An IndyCar steering wheel has more than a dozen buttons and a readout screen. The screen helps the driver keep track of engine temperature, oil levels, and fuel mileage. The buttons and switches let the driver make quick decisions about how to drive the car. One light indicates when it's time to switch gears.

Another lets the driver pick how the engine uses fuel. Sometimes it's best to put all the fuel into making the car go fast. Sometimes it's best to conserve energy and save on gas.

The king of steering wheels in racing is the Formula 1 wheel. It looks more like a game controller than a steering wheel. F1 drivers face tracks that can curve in any direction. The curves can be wide or tight. Because the course is always changing, drivers need to be able to make small, important changes to their car's performance. The F1 steering wheel has dozens of knobs, switches, and buttons. These buttons let the driver do everything from changing engine settings to readjusting the brakes. The technology of the steering wheel puts F1 drivers in complete control.

PIT CREW TECH

Pit stops take around 12 seconds for NASCAR. In that time, pit crews use top-of-the-line technology to get their cars back into top shape. Pneumatic air guns

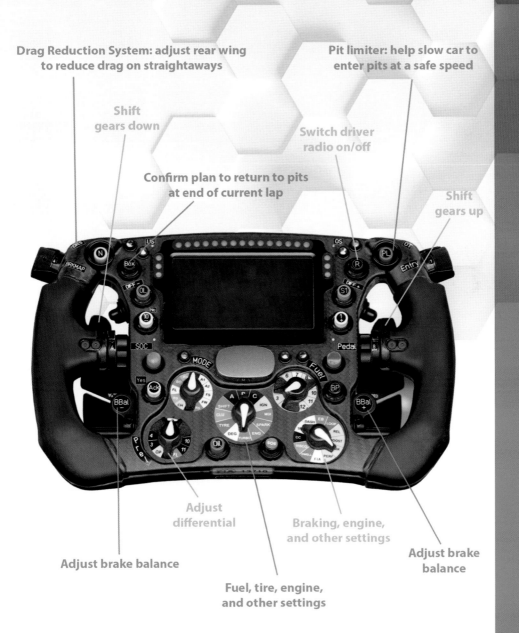

Drag Reduction System: adjust rear wing to reduce drag on straightaways

Shift gears down

Confirm plan to return to pits at end of current lap

Pit limiter: help slow car to enter pits at a safe speed

Switch driver radio on/off

Shift gears up

Adjust differential

Braking, engine, and other settings

Adjust brake balance

Adjust brake balance

Fuel, tire, engine, and other settings

The Formula 1 steering wheel is a feat of technology. Some buttons let the driver switch gears. Others let the driver control oil flow and fuel consumption. Switches let drivers change how the car handles corners, change engine modes, and much more.

F1 pit crews train hard to coordinate rapid, safe stops.

let them rapidly remove a tire's lug nuts and replace the tire. A crew member in a fireproof suit pours gasoline into the fuel tank.

While 12 seconds might seem fast, F1 pit stops are even quicker. F1 cars don't refuel at pit stops. They carry enough fuel for an entire race. The crew just has to swap out tires. A well-trained crew can get a car back on the road in just over two seconds.

PROTECTIVE TECH

Some technology doesn't come in the form of electronics or blinking lights. Sometimes technology is found in the types of materials used. For example, tires blew out frequently in the past. A blown-out tire could cause a car to spin out of control. To prevent spinouts, tire companies created a material that lines the inside of the tire. That way, even if the outside of the tire bursts, the inside remains inflated. That allows drivers to stop safely.

RACING TECH IN NORMAL CARS

Sometimes high-tech creations from the race track find their way into everyday cars. One example is disc-shaped brakes that started in race cars and are now standard in every car. A disc brake stops a car by squeezing a pair of pads against a metal disc. As the pads squeeze, they create friction. This stops the rotation of the wheels attached to the disc. The desire to create lighter, faster cars also led to the development of lighter materials. Lightweight, strong car bodies are a result of race car designers trying to drop as many pounds as possible.

Drivers work closely with engineers to get the most out of their cars.

4

ENGINEERING CARS AND TRACKS

Engineering is central to racing. The car has to be in good condition to compete. But engines aren't the only aspects of auto racing that are carefully engineered. Safety concerns also take center stage.

ENGINE AND HIGH SPEEDS

The heart of a race car is its engine. If the engine isn't working to its full potential,

Racing engines are efficient, lightweight, and very powerful.

the car won't have enough power to win a race. Because they are so important, it's no wonder careful engineering goes into each type of engine.

In a normal car, a lot of care goes into making engines work more quietly, vibrate less, and last a long time. For a racing engine, though, all focus is on making the engine lightweight and powerful. It doesn't have to last hundreds of thousands of miles like an engine in a normal car. It just has to last for one race at amazing speeds.

Racing officials have strict rules about how much a car must weigh. For example, IndyCars have to weigh at least 1,570 pounds (712 kg). The engine alone needs to be 248 pounds (112 kg). These engineering limits help level the playing field. Though cars can technically be heavier, most are as close to the minimum as possible.

NASCAR engines are built out of lightweight materials that are still incredibly strong. Race cars take so many turns at such high speeds that the car undergoes a lot of deformation. That means the car is compressing and stretching under the force of acceleration and turns. The engine faces stress from temperature and pressure. Engineers have created a material that can withstand these conditions. Most NASCAR engines are made out of compacted graphite iron. This material is strong but flexible. That makes it perfect for a car that makes so many high-speed turns.

BUILDING A SAFE CAR

Engineering plays a big role in creating a safe race. One major danger faced by drivers is, of course, crashes. With race cars moving at such high speeds, any kind of impact can cause major head or neck injuries. Because of this, safety engineers created the HANS device. HANS stands for Head and Neck Support. It is part of the helmet. It extends the helmet down the back of the neck. That way, the head and neck stay stable if there is a crash.

HYBRID CARS

Hybrid cars often get a bad reputation for being slow. A hybrid car uses both fuel and batteries for power. But Formula 1 racers have been racing hybrids since 2009. F1 has a restriction on how quickly an engine can use fuel. Slowing down fuel consumption puts a limit on how fast the car can go. To make up the speed, batteries help give an extra boost of power. F1 hybrids are far from slowpokes. They zoom around the track at speeds of more than 200 miles per hour (320 km/h).

HANS devices have been made mandatory in many types of auto racing.

A race car also has a strong seat belt setup. Most drivers use seat belts that have five or six straps. This is different from a normal car, which only has one strap that holds across the waist and chest. A NASCAR seat belt, for example, has straps for each shoulder, two that go across the waist, and at least one between the legs. These keep the chest and torso in place. The one between the legs keeps the driver from slipping out from under the seat belt.

The ultimate engineered safety measure is the roll cage. The roll cage is a protective frame built inside the car. This cage keeps the car from suffering too much damage as a result of a rollover crash. For example, support beams go from doors to the roof. That stops the roof from collapsing if there is a crash.

ENGINEERING SAFER TRACKS

To prevent crashes, engineers focus their efforts on more than the race cars. The track itself needs to be as safe as possible for both drivers and spectators. Because of this, engineers have put a lot of work into making safer barriers.

Many race tracks are surrounded by a thick wall. These barriers were once made out of concrete. However, a head-on crash into concrete could injure or even kill a driver. Researchers began intense studies that looked at barrier designs. They performed simulations and real-life test crashes to understand how different angles and speeds of impact affect a car.

A driver walks away unharmed from a collision with a wall.

DENSE FOAM TO ABSORB IMPACTS

HOLLOW STEEL WALL

STRAPS TO HELP HOLD STEEL WALL IN PLACE

CONCRETE WALL PROTECTS SPECTATORS

The SAFER barrier is made of multiple parts. The part the car directly impacts is made of a flexible steel. Inside the barrier, there is a strong foam. Both the steel and the foam change shape to absorb the energy of the crash. That way the car doesn't get bounced back out onto the track. This helps prevent a chain-reaction crash. The inside part of the barrier is concrete, which helps protect spectators.

In the end, they created the Steel and Foam Energy Reducing (SAFER) barrier. The SAFER barrier is covered with foam and has steel supports. The barrier absorbs some of the impact, so the crash force on the car and driver are reduced. The car is slowed down with less chance of bouncing back out onto the track. A high-speed crash is still dangerous, but less so with a softer barrier designed using STEM principles.

			BEST LAP	RAI	PER
1	3	RICCIARDO	1:49.930	+0.793	-19
2	26	KVYAT	1:49.980	32.362	307
3	5	VETTEL	1:50.460	31.179	336
4	33	VERSTAPPEN	1:50.599	32.316	307
5	44		1:50.635		294
6			1:50.707	30.998	335
			1:50.821		291
			1:51.104	31.234	337
			1:51.177	31.611	317
			1:51.378		
			1:51.531	31.203	340
			1.683		
			1.737	31.614	335
			2.025	31.577	336
			2.038	31.414	335
			2.289	31.303	332
			1:53.297	32.087	322
18			1:55.690	32.579	310
19			1:56.162	32.838	303
20					309

oup

MATH IN MOTION

Much of the math behind racing involves simple counting. The driver has to know how many cars are ahead of him. He has to know how many laps are left before the next pit stop or the end of the race. But racing involves more complex mathematics as well.

KEEPING A GRIP ON THE ROAD

Friction is the force generated when two objects rub together. When it comes to driving, friction is both bad and good.

Too much friction slows a car down. However, friction also keeps cars' wheels on the ground. The tires are designed to increase friction against the ground so that they don't spin out or slide around.

A NASCAR track might look like it's flat. But in fact, the turns on the tracks are angled. The inner edge is lower than the outer edge. This is called banking. If the road were totally flat, the cars would slide out if they tried to take a turn at full speed. Friction would not be enough to keep the tires firmly in contact with the ground.

Banking works because a road pushes back against the car. On a flat road, that push goes straight up. But on a banked road, the push is angled. Because a banked road is tilted toward the center of the track, it pushes the car back toward the center of the track. This extra push means the cars don't have to slow down as much to prevent themselves from sliding off the course.

Fans check out the banking at Daytona International Speedway.

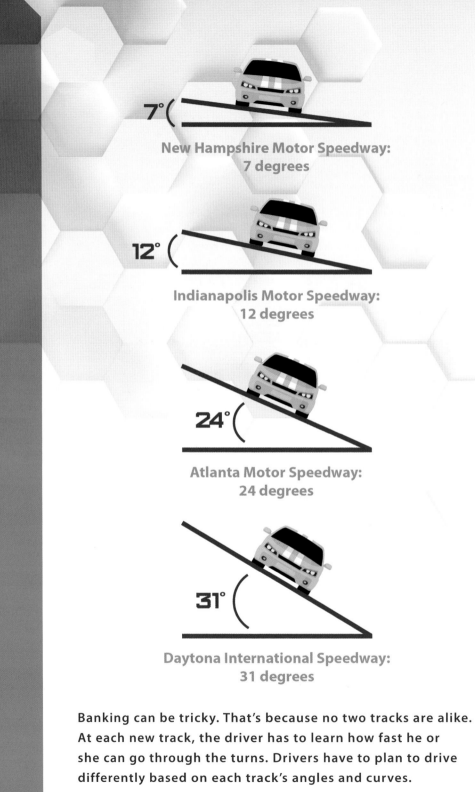

New Hampshire Motor Speedway:
7 degrees

Indianapolis Motor Speedway:
12 degrees

Atlanta Motor Speedway:
24 degrees

Daytona International Speedway:
31 degrees

Banking can be tricky. That's because no two tracks are alike. At each new track, the driver has to learn how fast he or she can go through the turns. Drivers have to plan to drive differently based on each track's angles and curves.

RACE TRACK BANKING

Calculating friction and banking is an important role for math in racing. Each track has a different angle of banking. For example, Daytona International Speedway in Daytona, Florida, banks at 31 degrees. That means the ground raises 31 degrees compared to the flat straightaways. But at New Hampshire Motor Speedway in Loudon, New Hampshire, the banking is only 7 degrees. A driver needs to know how fast she can push her car based on how high the banking is.

AIR PRESSURE IN TIRES

Tire pressure is a tricky business. When gas heats up, it expands. Friction causes heat. So as a car races around the track, the tires heat up to more than 200 degrees Fahrenheit (93°C). Under that kind of heat, the gas inside the tires will start to expand. Ordinary cars use the regular air we breathe in their tires. It contains nitrogen and oxygen. Racing cars use pure nitrogen. The tire holds its pressure for longer with nitrogen. And nitrogen expands less than regular air.

F1 teams can go through dozens of tires during each race.

Still, pit crews have to calculate tire pressure that takes expansion into consideration. They don't fill the tires all the way up. A NASCAR tire may actually look like it might be going flat as the race begins. In reality, that gas will expand to fill the tire before the race is done. Being able to calculate how much the gas will expand is key. If too much nitrogen is put into the tire initially, the tire may expand to the point of bursting.

STEM IN ACTION

An auto race is the ultimate show of STEM in action. Science and math help drivers understand the challenges of the track. Technology lets them have full control of their cars. Engineering is on display in the design of both cars and tracks. Skill and STEM combine to create thrilling experiences for drivers and fans at race tracks around the world.

TIMING A PIT STOP

A NASCAR pit stop is all about perfect timing, and that requires a lot of math. Pit crews need to keep track of how many more miles a set of tires can take. They also need to know how much fuel is left in the tank. When a car pulls in for a stop, the crew has to swap out tires, fill the tank, and clean the windshield and grille. And they have to do all of that in a matter of seconds.

GLOSSARY

AERODYNAMIC
Designed to minimize air resistance.

BARRIER
A wall that stops a car from leaving the track.

DEFORMATION
To be stretched or compressed into different shapes.

DIFFERENTIAL
A part in a car that allows the car's wheels to turn at different speeds.

INFLATE
To fill with a gas.

MOLECULE
A small building block of matter, such as oxygen or nitrogen.

PIT STOP
A break in a race where a car is refueled, fitted with new tires, and adjusted in other ways.

PNEUMATIC
Operated by air pressure.

TURBULENT
Irregularly moving air.

● ONLINE RESOURCES

Booklinks
NONFICTION NETWORK
FREE! ONLINE NONFICTION RESOURCES

To learn more about STEM in auto racing, visit **abdobooklinks.com.** These links are routinely monitored and updated to provide the most current information available.

● MORE INFORMATION

BOOKS

James, Brant. *Formula One Racing*. Minneapolis, MN: Abdo Publishing, 2015.

Long, Dustin. *NASCAR Racing*. Minneapolis, MN: Abdo Publishing, 2015.

Wilner, Barry. *The Best Auto Racers of All Time*. Minneapolis, MN: Abdo Publishing, 2015.

INDEX

ABOUT THE AUTHOR

Meg Marquardt started as a scientist but decided she liked writing about science even more. She enjoys researching physics, geology, and climate science. She lives in Madison, Wisconsin, with her two scientist cats, Lagrange and Doppler.